# Sea Snakes

by Colleen Sexton

BLASTOFF!
3
READERS

BELLWETHER MEDIA · MINNEAPOLIS, MN

Note to Librarians, Teachers, and Parents:

**Blastoff! Readers** are carefully developed by literacy experts and combine standards-based content with developmentally appropriate text.

**Level 1** provides the most support through repetition of high-frequency words, light text, predictable sentence patterns, and strong visual support.

**Level 2** offers early readers a bit more challenge through varied simple sentences, increased text load, and less repetition of high-frequency words.

**Level 3** advances early-fluent readers toward fluency through increased text and concept load, less reliance on visuals, longer sentences, and more literary language.

**Level 4** builds reading stamina by providing more text per page, increased use of punctuation, greater variation in sentence patterns, and increasingly challenging vocabulary.

**Level 5** encourages children to move from "learning to read" to "reading to learn" by providing even more text, varied writing styles, and less familiar topics.

Whichever book is right for your reader, Blastoff! Readers are the perfect books to build confidence and encourage a love of reading that will last a lifetime!

This edition first published in 2010 by Bellwether Media, Inc.

No part of this publication may be reproduced in whole or in part without written permission of the publisher. For information regarding permission, write to Bellwether Media, Inc., Attention: Permissions Department, 5357 Penn Avenue South, Minneapolis, MN 55419.

Library of Congress Cataloging-in-Publication Data

Sexton, Colleen.
  Sea snakes / by Colleen Sexton.
     p. cm. – (Blastoff! readers. Snakes alive!)
  Summary: "Simple text and full-color photography introduce beginning readers to sea snakes. Developed by literacy experts for students in kindergarten through third grade"–Provided by publisher.
  Includes bibliographical references and index.
  ISBN 978-1-60014-320-5 (hardcover : alk. paper)
  1. Sea snakes–Juvenile literature. I. Title.
  QL666.O64S492 2010
  597.96'5–dc22
                              2009037752

Text copyright © 2010 by Bellwether Media, Inc.
Printed in the United States of America, North Mankato, MN.
010110      1149

# Contents

What Are Sea Snakes? 4

Swimming and Breathing 9

Where Sea Snakes Live 14

Hunting and Feeding 16

Glossary 22

To Learn More 23

Index 24

Sea snakes are **poisonous** snakes that live in the ocean. There are more than 50 kinds of sea snakes.

Sea snakes come in
many colors and patterns.
Some are plain-colored.
Some have spots or stripes.

Sea snakes have small **scales**. Their skin can be smooth or rough.

Sea snakes **shed** their skin often to keep it clean and healthy.

Most sea snakes grow 3 to 5 feet (1 to 1.5 meters) long.

Sea snakes move their bodies
back and forth to swim. They steer
with their flat, paddle-shaped tails.

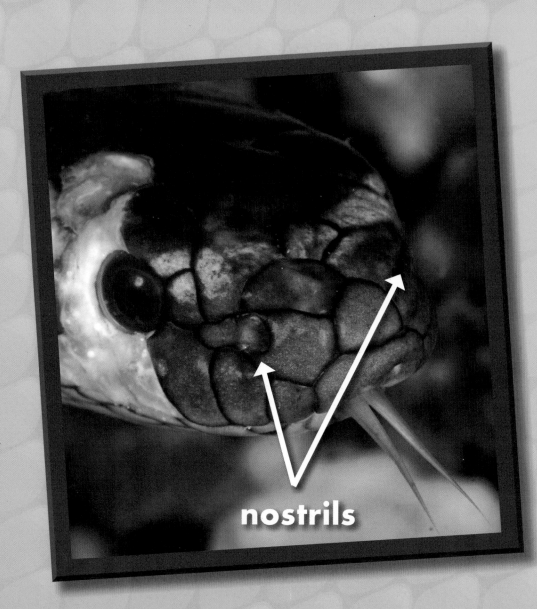

nostrils

Sea snakes have a small head with **nostrils** on top. The nostrils close to keep out water.

Sea snakes must swim to the surface for air. They open their nostrils to breathe.

Sea snakes have a small left **lung**. The right lung is nearly as long as the body. Breathing fills the long lung with air and helps the sea snake float.

Sea snakes can stay underwater for a long time. Many can hold their breath for more than an hour!

= areas where sea snakes live

Sea snakes live in the warm waters of the Indian and Pacific oceans. Most stay in **shallow** areas near land.

Yellow-bellied sea snakes **migrate** across deep parts of the ocean. They float in large groups and let the **current** carry them.

Sea snakes dive to the ocean floor to hunt.

They stick out their forked tongues to smell for eels and other **prey**.

eel

Most sea snakes eat fish and eels.
A few sea snakes eat only fish
eggs. They bite their prey with
sharp, hollow **fangs**.

A deadly poison called **venom** flows through the fangs and into the bite. Sea snakes swallow their prey whole.

Sea snakes get too much salt from their food. They have a special **gland** under their tongues where extra salt is stored.

Sea snakes need to get rid of the salt. They spit out a little salty water each time they stick out their tongues!

# Glossary

**current**—the movement of water in the ocean

**fangs**—sharp, curved teeth; sea snakes have short, hollow fangs through which venom can move into a bite.

**gland**—a body organ that takes a certain kind of matter out of the blood; the gland under a sea snake's tongue takes salt out of the blood.

**lung**—an organ inside the body that animals use to breathe air

**migrate**—to move from one place to another

**nostrils**—the openings of the nose

**poisonous**—able to kill or harm with a poison; the venom that a sea snake makes is a poison.

**prey**—an animal hunted by another animal for food

**scales**—small plates of skin that cover and protect a snake's body

**shallow**—not deep

**shed**—to let something fall off; sea snakes rub one part of their body against another part to help shed their skin.

**venom**—a poison that some snakes make; sea snake venom is deadly.

# To Learn More

**AT THE LIBRARY**

Gibbons, Gail. *Snakes*. New York, N.Y.: Holiday House, 2007.

Gunzi, Christiane. *The Best Book of Snakes*. New York, N.Y.: Kingfisher, 2003.

Patent, Dorothy Hinshaw. *Slinky, Scaly, Slithery Snakes*. New York, N.Y.: Walker & Co., 2000.

**ON THE WEB**

Learning more about sea snakes is as easy as 1, 2, 3.

1. Go to www.factsurfer.com.

2. Enter "sea snakes" into the search box.

3. Click the "Surf" button and you will see a list of related Web sites.

With factsurfer.com, finding more information is just a click away.

# Index

breathing, 11, 12, 13
colors, 5
current, 15
fangs, 18, 19
floating, 12, 15
forked tongues, 17, 20, 21
gland, 20
hunting, 16
Indian Ocean, 14
length, 8, 12
lung, 12
migration, 15
nostrils, 10, 11
ocean, 4, 14, 15, 16
Pacific Ocean, 14
patterns, 5
poison, 4, 19
prey, 17, 18, 19
salt, 20, 21

scales, 6
shedding, 7
skin, 6, 7
swallowing, 19
swimming, 9, 11
tails, 9
venom, 19
yellow-bellied sea snake, 15

The images in this book are reproduced through the courtesy of: Jez Tryner/imagequestmarine, front cover, p. 4 (small); Rodger Klein, pp. 4-5; Mike Turner, p. 6; Peter Arnold, Inc./Alamy, p. 7; Reinhard Dirscherl, p. 8; Gary Bell/Oceanwideimages.com, pp. 9, 12-13, 13 (small), 20-21; Mike Severns, p. 11; Jon Eppard, p. 14 (small); Darryl Leniuk, pp. 14-15; Tobais Bernhard, pp. 16-17; Juan Martinez, p. 17 (small); Brandon Cole, p. 18; SeaPics.com, p. 19.